Introduction

Hello! You may be feeling both anticipation and pressure as you think about your gap year. I want you to know that this in-between time doesn't have to be monumental or consistently productive, but it can be a time for you to get to know yourself a little better and prepare for what's next.

How to use this journal

I've included some prompts for writing, space for goal setting, and pages at the end for your notes. You might find it is helpful to create a ritual of writing at the same time each day. Some weeks you might also notice that you have fewer words or lose steam. That's ok! You have permission to be as descriptive or as terse as you feel.

Why the same prompt for a whole week?

Research shows that we learn through repetition and we can 'teach' our brains to notice the positives about our days. By paying attention to the same question for a whole week, you can build neural connections and mindfulness habits. Plus, it can show you that it is perfectly normal and maybe even beneficial that our perspectives can change day by day.

I wish you a wonderful year!

Katie

Plans for this year

JANUARY	FEBRUARY	MARCH

APRIL	MAY	JUNE

JULY	AUGUST	SEPTEMBER

OCTOBER	NOVEMBER	DECEMBER

Goals for the year

- 🌿 _____
- 🌿 _____
- 🌿 _____

- 🌿 _____
- 🌿 _____
- 🌿 _____

- 🌿 _____
- 🌿 _____
- 🌿 _____

week
1

What was unexpected about today?

monday:
_____
_____
_____
_____

tuesday:
_____
_____
_____
_____

wednesday:
_____
_____
_____
_____

thursday:
_____
_____
_____
_____

friday:

saturday:

sunday:

notes:

DATE _____

TOP 3 THINGS I DID THIS WEEK
○ _____
○ _____
○ _____

MOST REWARDING INTERACTION I
HAD THIS WEEK

THIS WEEK I FELT

NEXT WEEK I WANT TO _____

_____
_____
_____
_____

THINGS I ACCOMPLISHED THIS
WEEK

WHAT WAS A MEMORABLE
MOMENT FROM THE WEEK?

MY RANKING OF THE WEEK
☆ ☆ ☆ ☆ ☆

week
2

What did you make a priority today?

monday:
_____
_____
_____
_____

tuesday:
_____
_____
_____
_____

wednesday:
_____
_____
_____
_____

thursday:
_____
_____
_____
_____

friday:

saturday:

sunday:

notes:

Weekly review

DATE _____

TOP 3 THINGS I DID THIS WEEK
○ _____
○ _____
○ _____

THIS WEEK I FELT

NEXT WEEK I WANT TO _____

_____

_____

_____

_____

MOST REWARDING INTERACTION I HAD THIS WEEK

THINGS I ACCOMPLISHED THIS WEEK

WHAT WAS A MEMORABLE MOMENT FROM THE WEEK?

MY RANKING OF THE WEEK
☆ ☆ ☆ ☆ ☆

week
3

How did you show self-compassion today?

monday: _____
_____
_____
_____

tuesday: _____
_____
_____
_____

wednesday: _____
_____
_____
_____

thursday: _____
_____
_____
_____

friday:

_____

_____

_____

_____

saturday:

_____

_____

_____

_____

sunday:

_____

_____

_____

_____

notes:

_____

_____

_____

_____

_____

_____

Weekly review

DATE _____

TOP 3 THINGS I DID THIS WEEK

○ _____
○ _____
○ _____

THIS WEEK I FELT

NEXT WEEK I WANT TO

_____
_____
_____
_____

MOST REWARDING INTERACTION I HAD THIS WEEK

THINGS I ACCOMPLISHED THIS WEEK

WHAT WAS A MEMORABLE MOMENT FROM THE WEEK?

MY RANKING OF THE WEEK

☆ ☆ ☆ ☆ ☆

week
4

What did you read today?

monday:
_____
_____
_____
_____

tuesday:
_____
_____
_____
_____

wednesday:
_____
_____
_____
_____

thursday:
_____
_____
_____
_____

friday:

_____
_____
_____
_____

saturday:

_____
_____
_____

sunday:

_____
_____
_____

notes:

_____
_____
_____
_____
_____

DATE _____

TOP 3 THINGS I DID THIS WEEK

○ _____

○ _____

○ _____

THIS WEEK I FELT

MOST REWARDING INTERACTION I HAD THIS WEEK

NEXT WEEK I WANT TO

_____

_____

_____

_____

THINGS I ACCOMPLISHED THIS WEEK

WHAT WAS A MEMORABLE MOMENT FROM THE WEEK?

MY RANKING OF THE WEEK

☆ ☆ ☆ ☆ ☆

week
5

What was a conversation that you had today?

monday:
_____
_____
_____
_____

tuesday:
_____
_____
_____
_____

wednesday:
_____
_____
_____
_____

thursday:
_____
_____
_____
_____

friday:

_____

_____

_____

saturday:

_____

_____

_____

sunday:

_____

_____

_____

notes:

_____

_____

_____

_____

_____

Weekly review

DATE _____

TOP 3 THINGS I DID THIS WEEK

○ _____

○ _____

○ _____

THIS WEEK I FELT

NEXT WEEK I WANT TO

_____

_____

_____

_____

MOST REWARDING INTERACTION I HAD THIS WEEK

THINGS I ACCOMPLISHED THIS WEEK

WHAT WAS A MEMORABLE MOMENT FROM THE WEEK?

MY RANKING OF THE WEEK

☆ ☆ ☆ ☆ ☆

week
6

Where did you notice
kindness today?

monday:

_____

_____

_____

tuesday:

_____

_____

_____

wednesday:

_____

_____

_____

thursday:

_____

_____

_____

friday:

_____

_____

_____

_____

saturday:

_____

_____

_____

_____

sunday:

_____

_____

_____

_____

notes:

_____

_____

_____

_____

_____

_____

Weekly review

DATE _____

TOP 3 THINGS I DID THIS WEEK
○ _____
○ _____
○ _____

THIS WEEK I FELT

NEXT WEEK I WANT TO

_____
_____
_____
_____

MOST REWARDING INTERACTION I HAD THIS WEEK

THINGS I ACCOMPLISHED THIS WEEK

WHAT WAS A MEMORABLE MOMENT FROM THE WEEK?

MY RANKING OF THE WEEK

☆ ☆ ☆ ☆ ☆

week
7

What did you look forward to today?

monday: _____
_____
_____
_____

tuesday: _____
_____
_____
_____

wednesday: _____
_____
_____
_____

thursday: _____
_____
_____
_____

friday:

_____

_____

_____

_____

saturday:

_____

_____

_____

_____

sunday:

_____

_____

_____

_____

notes:

_____

_____

_____

_____

_____

_____

Weekly review

DATE _____

TOP 3 THINGS I DID THIS WEEK
- ○ _____
- ○ _____
- ○ _____

THIS WEEK I FELT

NEXT WEEK I WANT TO

_____

_____

_____

_____

MOST REWARDING INTERACTION I HAD THIS WEEK

THINGS I ACCOMPLISHED THIS WEEK

WHAT WAS A MEMORABLE MOMENT FROM THE WEEK?

MY RANKING OF THE WEEK

☆ ☆ ☆ ☆ ☆

week

8

What risk did you take today?

monday: _____
_____
_____
_____

tuesday: _____
_____
_____
_____

wednesday: _____
_____
_____
_____

thursday: _____
_____
_____
_____

friday:

_____

_____

_____

_____

saturday:

_____

_____

_____

_____

sunday:

_____

_____

_____

_____

notes:

_____

_____

_____

_____

_____

_____

Weekly review

DATE _____

TOP 3 THINGS I DID THIS WEEK
○ _____
○ _____
○ _____

THIS WEEK I FELT

MOST REWARDING INTERACTION I
HAD THIS WEEK

NEXT WEEK I WANT TO _____

_____
_____
_____
_____

THINGS I ACCOMPLISHED THIS
WEEK

WHAT WAS A MEMORABLE
MOMENT FROM THE WEEK?

MY RANKING OF THE WEEK

☆ ☆ ☆ ☆ ☆

week
9

What was today's tiny moment of joy?

monday:
_____
_____
_____
_____

tuesday:
_____
_____
_____

wednesday:
_____
_____
_____

thursday:
_____
_____
_____

friday:

saturday:

sunday:

notes:

DATE _____

TOP 3 THINGS I DID THIS WEEK
○ _____
○ _____
○ _____

MOST REWARDING INTERACTION I
HAD THIS WEEK

THIS WEEK I FELT

NEXT WEEK I WANT TO _____

_____
_____
_____
_____

THINGS I ACCOMPLISHED THIS
WEEK

WHAT WAS A MEMORABLE
MOMENT FROM THE WEEK?

MY RANKING OF THE WEEK
☆ ☆ ☆ ☆ ☆

week
10

What word describes
your day?

monday:
_____

_____

_____

_____

tuesday:
_____

_____

_____

_____

wednesday:
_____

_____

_____

_____

thursday:
_____

_____

_____

_____

friday:

saturday:

sunday:

notes:

DATE _____

TOP 3 THINGS I DID THIS WEEK
○ _____
○ _____
○ _____

THIS WEEK I FELT

MOST REWARDING INTERACTION I HAD THIS WEEK

NEXT WEEK I WANT TO
_____
_____
_____
_____

THINGS I ACCOMPLISHED THIS WEEK

WHAT WAS A MEMORABLE MOMENT FROM THE WEEK?

MY RANKING OF THE WEEK
☆ ☆ ☆ ☆ ☆

week
11

What did you accomplish today?

monday:
_____

_____

_____

tuesday:
_____

_____

_____

wednesday:
_____

_____

_____

thursday:
_____

_____

_____

friday:

saturday:

sunday:

notes:

DATE _____

TOP 3 THINGS I DID THIS WEEK
○ _____
○ _____
○ _____

THIS WEEK I FELT

NEXT WEEK I WANT TO _____

_____

_____

_____

_____

MOST REWARDING INTERACTION I
HAD THIS WEEK

THINGS I ACCOMPLISHED THIS
WEEK

WHAT WAS A MEMORABLE
MOMENT FROM THE WEEK?

MY RANKING OF THE WEEK
☆ ☆ ☆ ☆ ☆

week
12

What gave you a new perspective today?

monday:

_____

_____

_____

tuesday:

_____

_____

_____

wednesday:

_____

_____

_____

thursday:

_____

_____

_____

friday:

_____

_____

_____

saturday:

_____

_____

_____

sunday:

_____

_____

_____

notes:

_____

_____

_____

_____

_____

DATE _____

TOP 3 THINGS I DID THIS WEEK _____

○ _____

○ _____

○ _____

MOST REWARDING INTERACTION I
HAD THIS WEEK

THIS WEEK I FELT

NEXT WEEK I WANT TO _____

_____

_____

_____

_____

THINGS I ACCOMPLISHED THIS
WEEK

WHAT WAS A MEMORABLE
MOMENT FROM THE WEEK?

MY RANKING OF THE WEEK

☆ ☆ ☆ ☆ ☆

week
13

What did you want
more time for today?

monday:
_____
_____
_____
_____

tuesday:
_____
_____
_____
_____

wednesday:
_____
_____
_____
_____

thursday:
_____
_____
_____
_____

friday:

_____

_____

_____

_____

saturday:

_____

_____

_____

_____

sunday:

_____

_____

_____

_____

notes:

_____

_____

_____

_____

_____

_____

DATE _____

TOP 3 THINGS I DID THIS WEEK

○ _____

○ _____

○ _____

MOST REWARDING INTERACTION I HAD THIS WEEK

THIS WEEK I FELT

NEXT WEEK I WANT TO

_____

_____

_____

_____

THINGS I ACCOMPLISHED THIS WEEK

WHAT WAS A MEMORABLE MOMENT FROM THE WEEK?

MY RANKING OF THE WEEK

☆ ☆ ☆ ☆ ☆

week
14

Where did you notice empathy today?

monday: _____
_____
_____
_____

tuesday: _____
_____
_____
_____

wednesday: _____
_____
_____
_____

thursday: _____
_____
_____
_____

friday:

_____

_____

_____

saturday:

_____

_____

_____

sunday:

_____

_____

_____

notes:

_____

_____

_____

_____

_____

Weekly review

DATE _____

TOP 3 THINGS I DID THIS WEEK

○ _____

○ _____

○ _____

THIS WEEK I FELT

NEXT WEEK I WANT TO _____

MOST REWARDING INTERACTION I HAD THIS WEEK

_____

_____

_____

_____

THINGS I ACCOMPLISHED THIS WEEK

WHAT WAS A MEMORABLE MOMENT FROM THE WEEK?

MY RANKING OF THE WEEK

☆ ☆ ☆ ☆ ☆

week
15

What challenge did you overcame today?

monday:
_____
_____
_____

tuesday:
_____
_____
_____

wednesday:
_____
_____
_____

thursday:
_____
_____
_____

friday:
_____
_____
_____
_____

saturday:
_____
_____
_____
_____

sunday:
_____
_____
_____
_____

notes:
_____
_____
_____
_____
_____

Weekly review

DATE _____

TOP 3 THINGS I DID THIS WEEK

○ _____

○ _____

○ _____

THIS WEEK I FELT

NEXT WEEK I WANT TO

_____

MOST REWARDING INTERACTION I HAD THIS WEEK

THINGS I ACCOMPLISHED THIS WEEK

WHAT WAS A MEMORABLE MOMENT FROM THE WEEK?

MY RANKING OF THE WEEK

☆ ☆ ☆ ☆ ☆

week
16

What was your energy level today?

monday:
_____
_____
_____

tuesday:
_____
_____
_____

wednesday:
_____
_____
_____

thursday:
_____
_____
_____

friday:

_____

_____

_____

_____

saturday:

_____

_____

_____

_____

sunday:

_____

_____

_____

_____

notes:

_____

_____

_____

_____

_____

_____

Weekly review

DATE _____

TOP 3 THINGS I DID THIS WEEK

○ _____

○ _____

○ _____

THIS WEEK I FELT

NEXT WEEK I WANT TO

_____

_____

_____

_____

MOST REWARDING INTERACTION I HAD THIS WEEK

THINGS I ACCOMPLISHED THIS WEEK

WHAT WAS A MEMORABLE MOMENT FROM THE WEEK?

MY RANKING OF THE WEEK

☆ ☆ ☆ ☆ ☆

week
17

What were you confident about today?

monday: _____
_____
_____
_____

tuesday: _____
_____
_____
_____

wednesday: _____
_____
_____
_____

thursday: _____
_____
_____
_____

friday:

saturday:

sunday:

notes:

DATE _____

TOP 3 THINGS I DID THIS WEEK
○ _____
○ _____
○ _____

THIS WEEK I FELT

NEXT WEEK I WANT TO _____
_____
_____
_____
_____

MOST REWARDING INTERACTION I
HAD THIS WEEK

THINGS I ACCOMPLISHED THIS
WEEK

WHAT WAS A MEMORABLE
MOMENT FROM THE WEEK?

MY RANKING OF THE WEEK
☆ ☆ ☆ ☆ ☆

week
18

Who did you communicate with today?

monday:
_____
_____
_____
_____

tuesday:
_____
_____
_____
_____

wednesday:
_____
_____
_____
_____

thursday:
_____
_____
_____
_____

friday:

_____

_____

_____

_____

saturday:

_____

_____

_____

_____

sunday:

_____

_____

_____

_____

notes:

_____

_____

_____

_____

_____

_____

_____

DATE _____

TOP 3 THINGS I DID THIS WEEK _____

○ _____

○ _____

○ _____

THIS WEEK I FELT

MOST REWARDING INTERACTION I
HAD THIS WEEK

NEXT WEEK I WANT TO _____

_____

_____

_____

_____

THINGS I ACCOMPLISHED THIS
WEEK

WHAT WAS A MEMORABLE
MOMENT FROM THE WEEK?

MY RANKING OF THE WEEK

☆ ☆ ☆ ☆ ☆

week
19

How did social media make you feel today?

monday:

_____

_____

_____

_____

tuesday:

_____

_____

_____

wednesday:

_____

_____

_____

thursday:

_____

_____

_____

friday:

_____

_____

_____

saturday:

_____

_____

_____

sunday:

_____

_____

_____

notes:

_____

_____

_____

_____

_____

_____

DATE _____

TOP 3 THINGS I DID THIS WEEK
○ _____
○ _____
○ _____

THIS WEEK I FELT

NEXT WEEK I WANT TO _____

_____
_____
_____
_____

MOST REWARDING INTERACTION I HAD THIS WEEK

THINGS I ACCOMPLISHED THIS WEEK

WHAT WAS A MEMORABLE MOMENT FROM THE WEEK?

MY RANKING OF THE WEEK

☆ ☆ ☆ ☆ ☆

week
20

What is one decision
you made today?

monday:

_____

_____

_____

tuesday:

_____

_____

_____

wednesday:

_____

_____

_____

thursday:

_____

_____

_____

friday:

_____

_____

_____

saturday:

_____

_____

_____

sunday:

_____

_____

_____

notes:

_____

_____

_____

_____

_____

DATE _____

TOP 3 THINGS I DID THIS WEEK

○ _____

○ _____

○ _____

THIS WEEK I FELT

NEXT WEEK I WANT TO _____

_____

_____

_____

_____

MOST REWARDING INTERACTION I HAD THIS WEEK

THINGS I ACCOMPLISHED THIS WEEK

WHAT WAS A MEMORABLE MOMENT FROM THE WEEK?

MY RANKING OF THE WEEK

☆ ☆ ☆ ☆ ☆

week
21

How did your body feel today?

monday:

_____

_____

_____

tuesday:

_____

_____

_____

wednesday:

_____

_____

_____

thursday:

_____

_____

_____

friday:
_____
_____
_____
_____

saturday:
_____
_____
_____
_____

sunday:
_____
_____
_____
_____

notes:
_____
_____
_____
_____
_____
_____

Weekly review

DATE _____

TOP 3 THINGS I DID THIS WEEK

○ _____

○ _____

○ _____

THIS WEEK I FELT

NEXT WEEK I WANT TO

_____

_____

_____

_____

MOST REWARDING INTERACTION I HAD THIS WEEK

THINGS I ACCOMPLISHED THIS WEEK

WHAT WAS A MEMORABLE MOMENT FROM THE WEEK?

MY RANKING OF THE WEEK

☆ ☆ ☆ ☆ ☆

week
22

What did you create today?

monday:
_____
_____
_____
_____

tuesday:
_____
_____
_____

wednesday:
_____
_____
_____

thursday:
_____
_____
_____

friday:

_____

_____

_____

_____

saturday:

_____

_____

_____

_____

sunday:

_____

_____

_____

_____

notes:

_____

_____

_____

_____

_____

_____

Weekly review

DATE _____

TOP 3 THINGS I DID THIS WEEK

○ _____

○ _____

○ _____

THIS WEEK I FELT

NEXT WEEK I WANT TO

_____

_____

_____

_____

MOST REWARDING INTERACTION I HAD THIS WEEK

THINGS I ACCOMPLISHED THIS WEEK

WHAT WAS A MEMORABLE MOMENT FROM THE WEEK?

MY RANKING OF THE WEEK

☆ ☆ ☆ ☆ ☆

week
23

What is today's theme song?

monday:
_____
_____
_____
_____

tuesday:
_____
_____
_____

wednesday:
_____
_____
_____

thursday:
_____
_____
_____

friday:

_____

_____

_____

_____

saturday:

_____

_____

_____

_____

sunday:

_____

_____

_____

_____

notes:

_____

_____

_____

_____

_____

_____

DATE _____

TOP 3 THINGS I DID THIS WEEK
○ _____
○ _____
○ _____

MOST REWARDING INTERACTION I HAD THIS WEEK

THIS WEEK I FELT

NEXT WEEK I WANT TO _____

_____
_____
_____
_____

THINGS I ACCOMPLISHED THIS WEEK

WHAT WAS A MEMORABLE MOMENT FROM THE WEEK?

MY RANKING OF THE WEEK
☆ ☆ ☆ ☆ ☆

week
24

What obstacle did you face today?

monday:
_____

_____

_____

_____

tuesday:
_____

_____

_____

_____

wednesday:
_____

_____

_____

_____

thursday:
_____

_____

_____

_____

friday:

_____

_____

_____

saturday:

_____

_____

_____

sunday:

_____

_____

_____

notes:

_____

_____

_____

_____

_____

DATE _____

TOP 3 THINGS I DID THIS WEEK _____

○ _____

○ _____

○ _____

MOST REWARDING INTERACTION I
HAD THIS WEEK

THIS WEEK I FELT

NEXT WEEK I WANT TO _____

_____

_____

_____

_____

THINGS I ACCOMPLISHED THIS
WEEK

WHAT WAS A MEMORABLE
MOMENT FROM THE WEEK?

MY RANKING OF THE WEEK

☆ ☆ ☆ ☆ ☆

week
25

How did screen time affect you today?

monday:
_____
_____
_____
_____

tuesday:
_____
_____
_____

wednesday:
_____
_____
_____

thursday:
_____
_____
_____

friday:

_____

_____

_____

_____

saturday:

_____

_____

_____

_____

sunday:

_____

_____

_____

_____

notes:

_____

_____

_____

_____

_____

_____

Weekly review

DATE _____

TOP 3 THINGS I DID THIS WEEK

○ _____

○ _____

○ _____

THIS WEEK I FELT

MOST REWARDING INTERACTION I HAD THIS WEEK

NEXT WEEK I WANT TO

_____

_____

_____

_____

THINGS I ACCOMPLISHED THIS WEEK

WHAT WAS A MEMORABLE MOMENT FROM THE WEEK?

MY RANKING OF THE WEEK

☆ ☆ ☆ ☆ ☆

week
26

What about today would you do over?

monday:
_____
_____
_____
_____

tuesday:
_____
_____
_____
_____

wednesday:
_____
_____
_____
_____

thursday:
_____
_____
_____
_____

friday:

_____
_____
_____
_____

saturday:

_____
_____
_____
_____

sunday:

_____
_____
_____
_____

notes:

_____
_____
_____
_____
_____
_____

Weekly review

DATE _____

TOP 3 THINGS I DID THIS WEEK
○ _____
○ _____
○ _____

THIS WEEK I FELT

NEXT WEEK I WANT TO

_____
_____
_____
_____

THINGS I ACCOMPLISHED THIS WEEK

MOST REWARDING INTERACTION I HAD THIS WEEK

WHAT WAS A MEMORABLE MOMENT FROM THE WEEK?

MY RANKING OF THE WEEK
☆ ☆ ☆ ☆ ☆

week
27

What meme, song, or gif sums up today?

monday:

tuesday:

wednesday:

thursday:

friday:

_____

_____

_____

_____

saturday:

_____

_____

_____

_____

sunday:

_____

_____

_____

_____

notes:

_____

_____

_____

_____

_____

_____

_____

Weekly review

DATE _____

TOP 3 THINGS I DID THIS WEEK
○ _____
○ _____
○ _____

THIS WEEK I FELT

NEXT WEEK I WANT TO

_____
_____
_____
_____

MOST REWARDING INTERACTION I HAD THIS WEEK

THINGS I ACCOMPLISHED THIS WEEK

WHAT WAS A MEMORABLE MOMENT FROM THE WEEK?

MY RANKING OF THE WEEK
☆ ☆ ☆ ☆ ☆

week
28

What made you feel powerful today?

monday:

_____

_____

_____

tuesday:

_____

_____

_____

wednesday:

_____

_____

_____

thursday:

_____

_____

_____

friday:

saturday:

sunday:

notes:

Weekly review

DATE _____

TOP 3 THINGS I DID THIS WEEK _____

○ _____
○ _____
○ _____

THIS WEEK I FELT

MOST REWARDING INTERACTION I
HAD THIS WEEK

NEXT WEEK I WANT TO _____

_____
_____
_____
_____

THINGS I ACCOMPLISHED THIS
WEEK

WHAT WAS A MEMORABLE
MOMENT FROM THE WEEK?

MY RANKING OF THE WEEK
☆ ☆ ☆ ☆ ☆

week

29

What did you do to rest today?

monday:
_____
_____
_____
_____

tuesday:
_____
_____
_____
_____

wednesday:
_____
_____
_____
_____

thursday:
_____
_____
_____
_____

friday:

_____

_____

_____

_____

saturday:

_____

_____

_____

_____

sunday:

_____

_____

_____

_____

notes:

_____

_____

_____

_____

_____

_____

_____

DATE _____

TOP 3 THINGS I DID THIS WEEK _____

○ _____

○ _____

○ _____

THIS WEEK I FELT _____

NEXT WEEK I WANT TO _____

_____

_____

_____

_____

MOST REWARDING INTERACTION I HAD THIS WEEK _____

THINGS I ACCOMPLISHED THIS WEEK _____

WHAT WAS A MEMORABLE MOMENT FROM THE WEEK? _____

MY RANKING OF THE WEEK _____

☆ ☆ ☆ ☆ ☆

week
30

What about today was invigorating?

monday:

_____

_____

_____

tuesday:

_____

_____

_____

wednesday:

_____

_____

_____

thursday:

_____

_____

_____

friday:

_____

_____

_____

_____

saturday:

_____

_____

_____

_____

sunday:

_____

_____

_____

_____

notes:

_____

_____

_____

_____

_____

_____

DATE _____

TOP 3 THINGS I DID THIS WEEK _____

○ _____

○ _____

○ _____

MOST REWARDING INTERACTION I
HAD THIS WEEK _____

THIS WEEK I FELT

NEXT WEEK I WANT TO _____

_____

_____

_____

_____

THINGS I ACCOMPLISHED THIS
WEEK _____

WHAT WAS A MEMORABLE
MOMENT FROM THE WEEK? _____

MY RANKING OF THE WEEK _____

☆ ☆ ☆ ☆ ☆

week
31

How did people impact your day?

monday:
_____

_____

_____

_____

tuesday:
_____

_____

_____

_____

wednesday:
_____

_____

_____

_____

thursday:
_____

_____

_____

_____

friday:

_____

_____

_____

saturday:

_____

_____

_____

sunday:

_____

_____

_____

notes:

_____

_____

_____

_____

_____

DATE _____

TOP 3 THINGS I DID THIS WEEK _____

○ _____

○ _____

○ _____

THIS WEEK I FELT

MOST REWARDING INTERACTION I
HAD THIS WEEK

NEXT WEEK I WANT TO _____

_____

_____

_____

_____

THINGS I ACCOMPLISHED THIS
WEEK

WHAT WAS A MEMORABLE
MOMENT FROM THE WEEK?

MY RANKING OF THE WEEK

☆ ☆ ☆ ☆ ☆

week
32

Where did you find motivation today?

monday:

_____

_____

_____

tuesday:

_____

_____

_____

wednesday:

_____

_____

_____

thursday:

_____

_____

_____

friday:

saturday:

sunday:

notes:

Weekly review

DATE _____

TOP 3 THINGS I DID THIS WEEK _____

○ _____

○ _____

○ _____

THIS WEEK I FELT

NEXT WEEK I WANT TO _____

_____

_____

_____

_____

MOST REWARDING INTERACTION I
HAD THIS WEEK

THINGS I ACCOMPLISHED THIS
WEEK

WHAT WAS A MEMORABLE
MOMENT FROM THE WEEK?

MY RANKING OF THE WEEK

☆ ☆ ☆ ☆ ☆

week
33

How did you show patience today?

monday:
_____
_____
_____
_____

tuesday:
_____
_____
_____
_____

wednesday:
_____
_____
_____
_____

thursday:
_____
_____
_____
_____

friday:

_____

_____

_____

_____

saturday:

_____

_____

_____

_____

sunday:

_____

_____

_____

_____

notes:

_____

_____

_____

_____

_____

_____

_____

Weekly review

DATE _____

TOP 3 THINGS I DID THIS WEEK _____

○ _____

○ _____

○ _____

THIS WEEK I FELT _____

NEXT WEEK I WANT TO _____

_____

_____

_____

_____

MOST REWARDING INTERACTION I HAD THIS WEEK _____

THINGS I ACCOMPLISHED THIS WEEK _____

WHAT WAS A MEMORABLE MOMENT FROM THE WEEK? _____

MY RANKING OF THE WEEK _____

☆ ☆ ☆ ☆ ☆

week 34

What was something new that you tried today?

monday:

_____

_____

_____

tuesday:

_____

_____

_____

wednesday:

_____

_____

_____

thursday:

_____

_____

_____

friday:

_____
_____
_____
_____

saturday:

_____
_____
_____
_____

sunday:

_____
_____
_____
_____

notes:

_____
_____
_____
_____
_____
_____
_____

Weekly review

DATE _____

TOP 3 THINGS I DID THIS WEEK

○ _____

○ _____

○ _____

THIS WEEK I FELT

MOST REWARDING INTERACTION I HAD THIS WEEK

NEXT WEEK I WANT TO

_____

_____

_____

_____

THINGS I ACCOMPLISHED THIS WEEK

WHAT WAS A MEMORABLE MOMENT FROM THE WEEK?

MY RANKING OF THE WEEK

☆ ☆ ☆ ☆ ☆

Who did you help today?

monday:
_____
_____
_____
_____

tuesday:
_____
_____
_____
_____

wednesday:
_____
_____
_____
_____

thursday:
_____
_____
_____
_____

friday:

saturday:

sunday:

notes:

Weekly review

DATE _____

TOP 3 THINGS I DID THIS WEEK
○ _____
○ _____
○ _____

THIS WEEK I FELT

NEXT WEEK I WANT TO
_____
_____
_____
_____

MOST REWARDING INTERACTION I HAD THIS WEEK

THINGS I ACCOMPLISHED THIS WEEK

WHAT WAS A MEMORABLE MOMENT FROM THE WEEK?

MY RANKING OF THE WEEK
☆ ☆ ☆ ☆ ☆

week
36

What did you listen to today?

monday:

_____

_____

_____

_____

tuesday:

_____

_____

_____

wednesday:

_____

_____

_____

thursday:

_____

_____

_____

friday:

_____

_____

_____

_____

saturday:

_____

_____

_____

_____

sunday:

_____

_____

_____

_____

notes:

_____

_____

_____

_____

_____

_____

DATE _____

TOP 3 THINGS I DID THIS WEEK _____

○ _____

○ _____

○ _____

THIS WEEK I FELT

NEXT WEEK I WANT TO _____

_____

_____

_____

_____

MOST REWARDING INTERACTION I HAD THIS WEEK _____

THINGS I ACCOMPLISHED THIS WEEK _____

WHAT WAS A MEMORABLE MOMENT FROM THE WEEK? _____

MY RANKING OF THE WEEK _____

☆ ☆ ☆ ☆ ☆

week
37

What made you feel
proud today?

monday:

_____
_____
_____
_____

tuesday:

_____
_____
_____
_____

wednesday:

_____
_____
_____
_____

thursday:

_____
_____
_____
_____

friday:

_____

_____

_____

_____

saturday:

_____

_____

_____

_____

sunday:

_____

_____

_____

_____

notes:

_____

_____

_____

_____

_____

_____

_____

DATE _____

TOP 3 THINGS I DID THIS WEEK _____

○ _____

○ _____

○ _____

THIS WEEK I FELT

NEXT WEEK I WANT TO _____

_____

_____

_____

_____

MOST REWARDING INTERACTION I HAD THIS WEEK

THINGS I ACCOMPLISHED THIS WEEK

WHAT WAS A MEMORABLE MOMENT FROM THE WEEK?

MY RANKING OF THE WEEK

☆ ☆ ☆ ☆ ☆

week
38

What did you learn about yourself today?

monday:

_____

_____

_____

_____

tuesday:

_____

_____

_____

wednesday:

_____

_____

_____

thursday:

_____

_____

_____

friday:

_____

_____

_____

_____

saturday:

_____

_____

_____

_____

sunday:

_____

_____

_____

_____

notes:

_____

_____

_____

_____

_____

_____

_____

Weekly review

DATE _____

TOP 3 THINGS I DID THIS WEEK

○ _____

○ _____

○ _____

THIS WEEK I FELT

NEXT WEEK I WANT TO

_____

_____

_____

_____

MOST REWARDING INTERACTION I HAD THIS WEEK

THINGS I ACCOMPLISHED THIS WEEK

WHAT WAS A MEMORABLE MOMENT FROM THE WEEK?

MY RANKING OF THE WEEK

☆ ☆ ☆ ☆ ☆

week
39

What sparked your curiosity today?

monday:
_____
_____
_____
_____

tuesday:
_____
_____
_____
_____

wednesday:
_____
_____
_____
_____

thursday:
_____
_____
_____
_____

friday:

_____

_____

_____

_____

saturday:

_____

_____

_____

_____

sunday:

_____

_____

_____

_____

notes:

_____

_____

_____

_____

_____

_____

_____

DATE _____

TOP 3 THINGS I DID THIS WEEK _____

○ _____
○ _____
○ _____

THIS WEEK I FELT

NEXT WEEK I WANT TO _____

_____
_____
_____
_____

MOST REWARDING INTERACTION I
HAD THIS WEEK _____

THINGS I ACCOMPLISHED THIS
WEEK _____

WHAT WAS A MEMORABLE
MOMENT FROM THE WEEK? _____

MY RANKING OF THE WEEK _____

☆ ☆ ☆ ☆ ☆

week
40

How did you take care of yourself today?

monday:

_____

_____

_____

tuesday:

_____

_____

_____

wednesday:

_____

_____

_____

thursday:

_____

_____

_____

friday:

_____
_____
_____
_____

saturday:

_____
_____
_____
_____

sunday:

_____
_____
_____
_____

notes:

_____
_____
_____
_____
_____
_____

DATE _____

TOP 3 THINGS I DID THIS WEEK _____

○ _____

○ _____

○ _____

THIS WEEK I FELT

NEXT WEEK I WANT TO _____

_____

_____

_____

_____

MOST REWARDING INTERACTION I
HAD THIS WEEK _____

THINGS I ACCOMPLISHED THIS
WEEK _____

WHAT WAS A MEMORABLE
MOMENT FROM THE WEEK? _____

MY RANKING OF THE WEEK _____

☆ ☆ ☆ ☆ ☆

week
41

What was hard about today?

monday:

_____

_____

_____

tuesday:

_____

_____

_____

wednesday:

_____

_____

_____

thursday:

_____

_____

_____

friday:

_____

_____

_____

_____

saturday:

_____

_____

_____

_____

sunday:

_____

_____

_____

_____

notes:

_____

_____

_____

_____

_____

_____

_____

Weekly review

DATE _____

TOP 3 THINGS I DID THIS WEEK _____

○ _____

○ _____

○ _____

THIS WEEK I FELT _____

MOST REWARDING INTERACTION I HAD THIS WEEK _____

NEXT WEEK I WANT TO _____

_____

_____

_____

_____

THINGS I ACCOMPLISHED THIS WEEK _____

WHAT WAS A MEMORABLE MOMENT FROM THE WEEK? _____

MY RANKING OF THE WEEK _____

☆ ☆ ☆ ☆ ☆

week
42

How were you creative today?

monday:

_____

_____

_____

_____

tuesday:

_____

_____

_____

_____

wednesday:

_____

_____

_____

_____

thursday:

_____

_____

_____

_____

friday:

_____

_____

_____

_____

saturday:

_____

_____

_____

_____

sunday:

_____

_____

_____

_____

notes:

_____

_____

_____

_____

_____

_____

_____

DATE _____

TOP 3 THINGS I DID THIS WEEK _____

○ _____

○ _____

○ _____

THIS WEEK I FELT

MOST REWARDING INTERACTION I HAD THIS WEEK

NEXT WEEK I WANT TO _____

_____

_____

_____

_____

THINGS I ACCOMPLISHED THIS WEEK

WHAT WAS A MEMORABLE MOMENT FROM THE WEEK?

MY RANKING OF THE WEEK

☆ ☆ ☆ ☆ ☆

week
43

How did you leave your comfort zone today?

monday:
_____
_____
_____
_____

tuesday:
_____
_____
_____
_____

wednesday:
_____
_____
_____
_____

thursday:
_____
_____
_____
_____

friday:

_____
_____
_____
_____

saturday:

_____
_____
_____
_____

sunday:

_____
_____
_____
_____

notes:

_____
_____
_____
_____
_____
_____
_____

Weekly review

DATE _____

TOP 3 THINGS I DID THIS WEEK

○ _____

○ _____

○ _____

THIS WEEK I FELT

NEXT WEEK I WANT TO _____

_____

_____

_____

_____

MOST REWARDING INTERACTION I HAD THIS WEEK

THINGS I ACCOMPLISHED THIS WEEK

WHAT WAS A MEMORABLE MOMENT FROM THE WEEK?

MY RANKING OF THE WEEK

☆ ☆ ☆ ☆ ☆

week
44

What did you make time for today?

monday:

_____

_____

_____

tuesday:

_____

_____

_____

wednesday:

_____

_____

_____

thursday:

_____

_____

_____

friday:

_____

_____

_____

_____

saturday:

_____

_____

_____

_____

sunday:

_____

_____

_____

_____

notes:

_____

_____

_____

_____

_____

_____

_____

Weekly review

DATE _____

TOP 3 THINGS I DID THIS WEEK _____

○ _____

○ _____

○ _____

THIS WEEK I FELT _____

NEXT WEEK I WANT TO _____

_____

_____

_____

_____

MOST REWARDING INTERACTION I HAD THIS WEEK _____

THINGS I ACCOMPLISHED THIS WEEK _____

WHAT WAS A MEMORABLE MOMENT FROM THE WEEK? _____

MY RANKING OF THE WEEK _____

☆ ☆ ☆ ☆ ☆

week
45

What about today felt peaceful?

monday:

_____

_____

_____

tuesday:

_____

_____

_____

wednesday:

_____

_____

_____

thursday:

_____

_____

_____

friday:

saturday:

sunday:

notes:

DATE _____

TOP 3 THINGS I DID THIS WEEK

○ _____

○ _____

○ _____

THIS WEEK I FELT

MOST REWARDING INTERACTION I
HAD THIS WEEK

NEXT WEEK I WANT TO

_____

_____

_____

_____

THINGS I ACCOMPLISHED THIS
WEEK

WHAT WAS A MEMORABLE
MOMENT FROM THE WEEK?

MY RANKING OF THE WEEK

☆ ☆ ☆ ☆ ☆

week
46

Who was on your mind today?

monday:
_____
_____
_____
_____

tuesday:
_____
_____
_____

wednesday:
_____
_____
_____

thursday:
_____
_____
_____

friday:

_____

_____

_____

_____

saturday:

_____

_____

_____

_____

sunday:

_____

_____

_____

_____

notes:

_____

_____

_____

_____

_____

_____

_____

Weekly review

DATE _____

TOP 3 THINGS I DID THIS WEEK _____

○ _____

○ _____

○ _____

THIS WEEK I FELT

MOST REWARDING INTERACTION I
HAD THIS WEEK _____

NEXT WEEK I WANT TO _____

_____

_____

_____

_____

THINGS I ACCOMPLISHED THIS
WEEK _____

WHAT WAS A MEMORABLE
MOMENT FROM THE WEEK? _____

MY RANKING OF THE WEEK _____

☆ ☆ ☆ ☆ ☆

week
47

What goal did you work towards today?

monday:

_____

_____

_____

tuesday:

_____

_____

_____

wednesday:

_____

_____

_____

thursday:

_____

_____

_____

friday:

_____

_____

_____

_____

saturday:

_____

_____

_____

_____

sunday:

_____

_____

_____

_____

notes:

_____

_____

_____

_____

_____

_____

Weekly review

DATE _____

TOP 3 THINGS I DID THIS WEEK
○ _____

○ _____

○ _____

THIS WEEK I FELT

NEXT WEEK I WANT TO _____

_____

_____

_____

_____

MOST REWARDING INTERACTION I
HAD THIS WEEK

THINGS I ACCOMPLISHED THIS
WEEK

WHAT WAS A MEMORABLE
MOMENT FROM THE WEEK?

MY RANKING OF THE WEEK
☆ ☆ ☆ ☆ ☆

week
48

What was your self
care like today?

monday:
_____
_____
_____
_____

tuesday:
_____
_____
_____
_____

wednesday:
_____
_____
_____
_____

thursday:
_____
_____
_____
_____

friday:

_____
_____
_____

saturday:

_____
_____
_____

sunday:

_____
_____
_____

notes:

_____
_____
_____
_____
_____
_____

DATE _____

TOP 3 THINGS I DID THIS WEEK _____

○ _____

○ _____

○ _____

THIS WEEK I FELT

NEXT WEEK I WANT TO _____

_____

_____

_____

_____

MOST REWARDING INTERACTION I HAD THIS WEEK

THINGS I ACCOMPLISHED THIS WEEK

WHAT WAS A MEMORABLE MOMENT FROM THE WEEK?

MY RANKING OF THE WEEK

☆ ☆ ☆ ☆ ☆

week
49

What made you laugh today?

monday: _____
_____
_____
_____

tuesday: _____
_____
_____
_____

wednesday: _____
_____
_____
_____

thursday: _____
_____
_____
_____

friday:

_____

_____

_____

saturday:

_____

_____

_____

sunday:

_____

_____

_____

notes:

_____

_____

_____

_____

_____

_____

Weekly review

DATE _____

TOP 3 THINGS I DID THIS WEEK

○ _____

○ _____

○ _____

THIS WEEK I FELT

NEXT WEEK I WANT TO _____

_____

_____

_____

_____

THINGS I ACCOMPLISHED THIS WEEK

MOST REWARDING INTERACTION I HAD THIS WEEK

WHAT WAS A MEMORABLE MOMENT FROM THE WEEK?

MY RANKING OF THE WEEK

☆ ☆ ☆ ☆ ☆

week
50

What helped you today?

monday:

_____

_____

_____

_____

tuesday:

_____

_____

_____

wednesday:

_____

_____

_____

thursday:

_____

_____

_____

friday:

saturday:

sunday:

notes:

Weekly review

DATE _____

TOP 3 THINGS I DID THIS WEEK

- ○ _____
- ○ _____
- ○ _____

THIS WEEK I FELT

NEXT WEEK I WANT TO

_____

_____

_____

_____

MOST REWARDING INTERACTION I HAD THIS WEEK

THINGS I ACCOMPLISHED THIS WEEK

WHAT WAS A MEMORABLE MOMENT FROM THE WEEK?

MY RANKING OF THE WEEK

☆ ☆ ☆ ☆ ☆

week

51

What made your
heart happy today?

monday:
_____
_____
_____

tuesday:
_____
_____
_____

wednesday:
_____
_____
_____

thursday:
_____
_____
_____

friday:

_____

_____

_____

saturday:

_____

_____

_____

sunday:

_____

_____

_____

notes:

_____

_____

_____

_____

_____

DATE _____

TOP 3 THINGS I DID THIS WEEK _____

○ _____

○ _____

○ _____

THIS WEEK I FELT

MOST REWARDING INTERACTION I
HAD THIS WEEK _____

NEXT WEEK I WANT TO _____

_____

_____

_____

_____

THINGS I ACCOMPLISHED THIS
WEEK _____

WHAT WAS A MEMORABLE
MOMENT FROM THE WEEK? _____

MY RANKING OF THE WEEK _____

☆ ☆ ☆ ☆ ☆

week
52

What would your childhood self think about today?

monday:
_____
_____
_____
_____

tuesday:
_____
_____
_____
_____

wednesday:
_____
_____
_____
_____

thursday:
_____
_____
_____
_____

friday:

saturday:

sunday:

notes:

Weekly review

DATE _____

TOP 3 THINGS I DID THIS WEEK

○ _____

○ _____

○ _____

THIS WEEK I FELT

MOST REWARDING INTERACTION I HAD THIS WEEK

NEXT WEEK I WANT TO

_____

_____

_____

_____

THINGS I ACCOMPLISHED THIS WEEK

WHAT WAS A MEMORABLE MOMENT FROM THE WEEK?

MY RANKING OF THE WEEK

☆ ☆ ☆ ☆ ☆

(For extra days)

week 53

What felt satisfying about today?

monday:

tuesday:

wednesday:

thursday:

friday:

_____

_____

_____

_____

saturday:

_____

_____

_____

_____

sunday:

_____

_____

_____

_____

notes:

_____

_____

_____

_____

_____

_____

Weekly review

DATE _____

TOP 3 THINGS I DID THIS WEEK _____

○ _____

○ _____

○ _____

THIS WEEK I FELT

NEXT WEEK I WANT TO _____

_____

_____

_____

_____

MOST REWARDING INTERACTION I
HAD THIS WEEK

THINGS I ACCOMPLISHED THIS
WEEK

WHAT WAS A MEMORABLE
MOMENT FROM THE WEEK?

MY RANKING OF THE WEEK

☆ ☆ ☆ ☆ ☆

Printed in Great Britain
by Amazon

25023593R00126